Family Literacy

Easy Ways for Families to Read and Write Together

by Marcia Ardis

Literacy Links
8 Larkmoor Drive
P.O. Box 77
Glen Carbon, IL 62034
http://www.literacylinks.com

Literacy Links
8 Larkmoor Drive
P.O. Box 77
Glen Carbon, IL 62034

ISBN 0-9667936-1-7

For information about REPRODUCIBLE BLACKLINE MASTERS
of Literacy Links' materials, see page 96
or visit our web site at www.literacylinks.com.

Author: Marcia Ardis
Illustrator: Linda Johnson
Cover Design: Greg Myers, Ann Martin
Editor and CEH: Colby Ardis
Published by Literacy Links
Printed in the United States of America

Publication Office:
P.O. Box 77
Glen Carbon, IL 62034

Business Office:
8 Larkmoor Drive
Suite 2
Glen Carbon, IL 62034
Telephone: (618) 288-4999
Fax: (618) 288-7175
E-mail: marcia@literacylinks.com
Web site: www.literacylinks.com

Table of Contents

WELCOME LETTER

Dear Parent, Teacher, Significant Adult and Caregiver,

Everyday family life is busy! Do you wonder "How can we find time to emphasize the importance of reading and writing? How can we provide our children with the experiences they need to be successful readers and writers?"

FAMILY LITERACY: EASY WAYS FOR FAMILIES TO READ AND WRITE TOGETHER will help you "sprinkle" reading and writing experiences throughout your busy days. Literacy (reading, writing, listening, speaking and thinking) can be a part of every waking moment of every day. You don't need to schedule sit-down study time. Rather, use some of the ideas in this book to "sprinkle" literacy throughout your day in natural ways.

This book includes

- ♥ Numerous ideas on every page that you can use to read and write with children

- ♥ Journal writing pages that allow families to record their reading and writing experiences

- ♥ Activities that encourage thinking while engaging in literacy experiences with ABC's

- ♥ Easy-to-understand explanations of how children learn to listen, speak, read and write

- ♥ A message on the importance of reading aloud to children

I encourage you to find the "village of people" who spend time with your young children. Invite these people to talk, sing, read, write, listen and speak to your children. As a team, you are your children's first teachers. Be proud of what you can do together. Enjoy literacy. Create lifelong readers and writers. Begin early ... Begin NOW.

God bless you in all that you do!

Marcia Ardis

Marcia Ardis

Few children

learn to love books

by themselves.

Someone has to lure them

into the wonderful world

of the written word.

Someone has to show them the way.

Orville Prescott

from <u>A Father Reads to His Children</u>

Language and Literacy:

Reading, Writing, Listening, Speaking and Thinking

Language begins to develop when your baby hears spoken language.

Talk, chant, sing and rhyme with your children (from infancy on) to nurture language development.

Find time to read, write, speak and listen to and with your children.

Encourage others to read, write, speak and listen to and with your children.

Read aloud to children of all ages.

Find spontaneous ways to include reading, writing, listening and speaking in your everyday lives.
(ways to use language without taking additional time)

Think about what you did with language when you were a child.
Pass on those language traditions and activities to your children.

Immersing your children in language experiences in their earliest years provides a firm foundation for strong language development.

While reading to my young son,

I noticed that he was getting drowsy.

As I started to put the book away,

he awoke enough to say,

"Don't stop, Daddy.

Sometimes my ears stay up later than my eyes."

Author Unknown

THE IMPORTANCE OF
READING ALOUD TO CHILDREN

Many of the ideas in this book are centered around books.
Find time to read aloud to your children every day.
Encourage the people who spend time with your children
to read aloud to them.

Reading Aloud . . .

Stimulates your children's imaginations

Develops interest in reading and in books

Improves your children's listening skills

Builds vocabulary

Helps your children to understand stories and book language

Creates a bond between you and your children

Provides your children with positive role models

Helps children to become independent readers

Reading aloud to your children
may be the best family activity
that allows your children
to reach their potential in learning.

FAMILY
LITERACY
JOURNAL
AND
ACTIVITIES

Take time to read, write, listen, speak and think together. The time you take, and the experiences that you have, are an investment in your children's futures. As a family, record your experiences on these journal pages. This family literacy journal will serve as a reminder of time well spent and experiences that may become traditional in your family.

Books, Books, Books

Color one book
each time you have
a quiet reading time at home.

Make a GOOD HABIT ... Read every day!

Set a goal ... _____ books per month

Books, Books, Books

Put books in all rooms of your house...

♥ in the bedroom next to your children's beds

♥ in the bathroom

♥ in the kitchen

♥ on the floor next to the TV (Which is more important?)

♥ on the table ... Clutter the table with books

Encourage your children to read
whenever they have some "quiet time."

Set a timer for 30 minutes each night
for quiet reading and writing time.

Encourage your children to read in bed
before they go to sleep.
Let them keep "lights on"
for 15 minutes past their bedtimes.

Books, Books
And More Books

Name some places that you travel to in your car.

Color the READ license plate when you read
while traveling to that place.

_____

_____

_____

_____

_____

Books, Books And More Books

Put BOOKS in your car.
Always take BOOKS with you as you travel.

♥ When you stop for an appointment (doctor, dentist), take some BOOKS with you to READ as you wait.

♥ When you are taking a long trip in the car, have BOOKS with you.

♥ When you are delayed in traffic, READ and encourage your children to READ.

♥ When you are waiting to meet someone, READ.

♥ When you know that you will have to wait in line (grocery store, post office, etc.), have a BOOK with you to READ to your children.

READ, READ, READ ...
You serve as a GREAT ROLE MODEL to your children and to others!!!

Read Aloud

Write the titles of the books that you read.
Color the ☺ ☺ ☺ to tell how much you liked the book.

☺   good book
☺ ☺   great book
☺ ☺ ☺   awesome book

_____   ☺ ☺ ☺

_____   ☺ ☺ ☺

_____   ☺ ☺ ☺

_____   ☺ ☺ ☺

_____   ☺ ☺ ☺

_____   ☺ ☺ ☺

_____   ☺ ☺ ☺

_____   ☺ ☺ ☺

_____   ☺ ☺ ☺

_____   ☺ ☺ ☺

Read Aloud

Read aloud to your children every day.

Read books that are ABOVE your children's reading levels.

Read aloud to children of ALL ages.

Reading aloud to your children:

- ♥ stimulates your children's imaginations
- ♥ develops interest in reading and in books
- ♥ improves your children's listening skills
- ♥ builds vocabulary
- ♥ helps your children understand stories and book language
- ♥ creates a bond between you and your children
- ♥ provides your children with a positive role model
- ♥ helps children become independent readers

Reading Partners

These people read a book to me!

_____

_____

_____

_____

_____

_____

_____

_____

Reading Partners

Make a list of the people who spend time with your children.

Your list might include:

- ♥ Day care, nursery school or baby sitter
- ♥ Aunt
- ♥ Uncle
- ♥ Grandma
- ♥ Grandpa
- ♥ Neighbor
- ♥ Friend

Ask these people to read at least
one book to your children
when they are spending time together.

Reread Favorite Books

List the titles of your favorite books.
Tell why each book is a favorite.

_____ is a favorite

book because _____

_____

_____ is a favorite

book because _____

_____

_____ is a favorite

book because _____

_____

_____ is a favorite

book because _____

_____

Reread Favorite Books

Rereading favorite books is an important experience for young children.
Children become confident and begin to see themselves as readers when they are comfortable with their favorite books.

As you reread the favorites ...

- ♥ Lightly touch the words as you read together.

- ♥ Encourage your children to "echo read" (read along with you).

- ♥ Find favorite words. Find words that are repeated in the book.

- ♥ Talk about the sounds and letters at the beginning and end of words.

- ♥ Notice the pictures.

- ♥ Stop to talk about the story as you are reading together.

What Are We Reading?

Our Reading List

Name	What We Are Reading

Give rewards for achieving goals!

What Are We Reading?

Keep a list of the books, magazines, newspapers, etc. that everyone in your family is reading.

Helpful hints in keeping this list:

♥ Keep the list posted in a convenient place and in a place where it will be seen often (on the refrigerator, on the book shelf, next to the telephone).

♥ Encourage every family member to add to the list.

♥ Encourage people who visit your home to add to the list.

♥ Include books, magazines, newspapers, etc.

♥ When a page is filled, save it.

♥ Comment on how proud you are of everyone and how quickly the list is growing.

Minutes of Reading

NAME	MINUTES OF READING						TOTAL

CELEBRATION: _____

Minutes of Reading

Chart the number of minutes your family reads each day. Plan a simple celebration when your family reaches a certain number of minutes.

Helpful hints:

♥ Encourage each family member to decide how many minutes of reading he/she will complete.

♥ Add these minutes together to set your family's goal for the week.

♥ Decide ahead of time what the celebration will be. This gives everyone something to look forward to.

♥ Allow your children to design the chart that they will use to keep track of the number of minutes of family reading.

Visit the Public Library

What do you like to read and learn about?

_____ (sports)

_____ (animals)

_____ (storybooks)

_____ (poems)

_____ (songs)

_____ (hobbies)

_____ (mysteries)

_____ (science)

_____ (people)

_____ (special events)

_____ (other)

Visit the Public Library

A visit to the public library can result in hours of time spent reading and enjoying good books.

- Visit the library at least one time each month. If you cannot take your children, ask a relative or friend to help.

- Ask your library for a list of the books that your children check out. If the library cannot give you a list, have your children write down the titles.

- Allow each child to check out a certain number of books. Write down the number of books on your calendar so that everyone knows how many books need to be returned and when to return them.

- Plan to visit the library on special occasions ... for a birthday or holiday, as a reward for finishing homework or chores, as part of a slumber party or family gathering.

Magazine Collections

Find 5 people who would like
to start a magazine swap.

1. _____

2. _____

3. _____

4. _____

5. _____

What kinds of magazines do
they like to read?

1. _____

2. _____

3. _____

4. _____

5. _____

Collect magazines from these 5 people and from
others. Get together each month to swap
magazines.

Magazine Collections

Encourage your children
to collect used magazines
for their own use
and to give to others.

Have your children use magazines
in the following ways:

♥ Collect magazines from relatives, friends and neighbors.

♥ Sort the magazines according to topics (Sports, Gardening,
  Crafts, Finances, etc.)

♥ Give magazines to others. First, ask them about their
  interests. Then, select some magazines that they would enjoy
  reading.

Dictionary Fun

List your "Words of the Day."
Encourage everyone in your family
to use the words.

_____

_____

_____

_____

_____

_____

_____

_____

_____

_____

Dictionary Fun

Keep a children's dictionary in a handy place so that it can be used regularly and often.

Helpful hints on encouraging your children to use the dictionary:

♥ Encourage your children to choose a "Word of the Day." Talk about what the word means. Use it in a sentence. See how many times everyone can use it during the day.

♥ Find categories of words using words from the dictionary. For example, look for words that name animals; words that name things that are cold; words that begin with the letter ___ ; words that have little words in them.

♥ Use the dictionary when your children ask you what a word means or how to spell a word.

Reading Signs

Draw and label some of the signs that you notice when you are traveling around town.

Reading Signs

When you travel around town or long distance, notice the signs around you.

♥ Road signs

♥ Street signs

♥ Store signs

♥ Restaurant signs

♥ Billboards and advertisements

♥ Directions

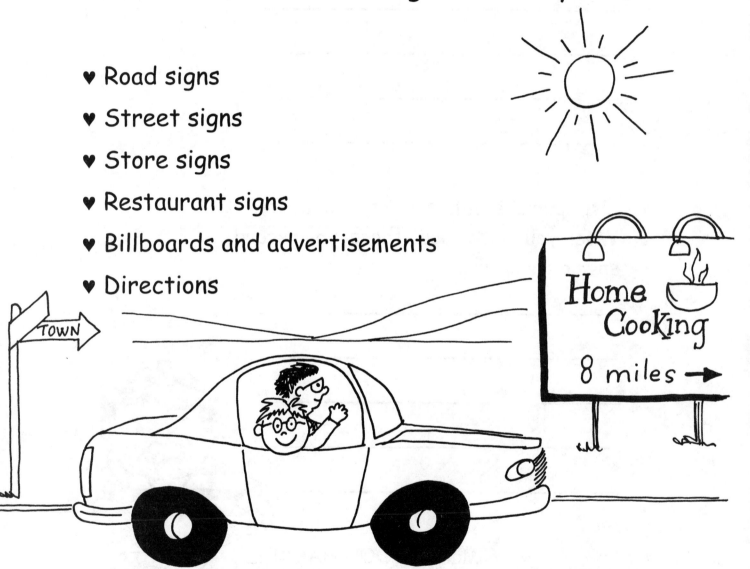

Give your children paper and markers to design signs.
Post the signs that they design around your home.

Journal Writing

List topics that you like to write about.

_____

_____

_____

_____

List special events that you celebrate.
When you write about these, you record
special memories.

_____

_____

_____

_____

_____

Make a GOOD HABIT ...
Write in your journal every day!

Journal Writing

Give your children a notebook or pad of paper to use as a journal.

- ♥ Encourage your children to write in the journal every day or at least a few times each week.

- ♥ Setting up a special time each evening for journal writing allows writing to become a habit.

- ♥ Reread and enjoy what was written the previous week, month, or year. The effort of writing becomes a treasured experience as you relive old memories.

- ♥ Add comments to your children's journals. Choose pages that you especially like and write a comment or write a question about what they shared.

Draw and Tell

Draw your family and tell about them.

_____

_____

_____

_____

_____

Draw and Tell

After your children draw pictures, ask them to tell you about the pictures. Write what they say at the bottom of the picture.

This "Draw and Tell" approach:

♥ Allows children to be creative while drawing and talking about their pictures.

♥ Allows children to see you write their spoken words. This helps them to understand the beginning stages of writing and spelling.

♥ Gives your family a collection of pictures and sentences to read and reread. This helps children to understand the beginning stages of reading and gives your children pages that they can read with you.

Family Mailbox

Make a list of the
"Mail Person of the Week."

Take turns, allowing each person
in your family to deliver mail.

Week 1 _____

Week 2 _____

Week 3 _____

Week 4 _____

Week 5 _____

Week 6 _____

Week 7 _____

Week 8 _____

Family Mailbox

Have a family mailbox that everyone can use to write notes to each other.

♥ Create a family mailbox using a shoe box, cereal box or small gift box.

♥ Decorate it and put your house number on it.

♥ Use this family mailbox to send messages to each other.

♥ Appoint a "mail person" of the day (or week) to deliver the mail to each person in the family.

♥ Place special mail (birthday cards, special occasion mail) in this family mailbox.

♥ When you receive mail from a family member, write back to that person. This note writing encourages reading and writing.

Thank You Notes

Keep a record of who sent you gifts and who you want to thank for doing something special for you. After you send a thank you note, color the ☺.

Gift or "Something Special"	Sender	☺
		☺
_____	_____	☺
_____	_____	☺
_____	_____	☺
_____	_____	☺
_____	_____	☺
_____	_____	☺
_____	_____	☺
_____	_____	☺

Thank You Notes

Encourage your children to send thank you cards when they receive gifts.

These ideas may help provide motivation:

♥ Have paper, markers, pencils, envelopes and postage stamps in a box marked "Cards." It saves time and creates interest when the "tools" are conveniently organized.

♥ Expect your children to write thank you cards for gifts that they receive. Once a habit is in place, it will continue in an easy fashion.

♥ Allow your preschool children to tell you what to write on the cards that they illustrate. This begins the habit of card making at an early age. Also, it gives your children an opportunity to see their thoughts and words in print.

♥ Have your children design some cards illustrating the front of each card and writing a simple verse on the inside. Use a copy machine to make many copies of each card. When a card needs to be sent, the children can choose from among the ones they made, add a personal message and send the card.

♥ When children are given money as a gift, expect them to send a thank you card BEFORE they spend the money.

♥ When given money as a gift, encourage your children to buy one good book with some of the money.

List Making

Use this grocery store list.

FRUITS AND VEGETABLES	DAIRY FOODS	MEAT
_____	_____	_____
_____	_____	_____
_____	_____	_____

CANNED FOODS	FROZEN FOODS	SNACKS
_____	_____	_____
_____	_____	_____
_____	_____	_____

PAPER PRODUCTS	CLEANING PRODUCTS	EXTRAS
_____	_____	_____
_____	_____	_____
_____	_____	_____

MAKE YOUR OWN LIST IN THE AISLE ORDER YOU USE AT YOUR GROCERY STORE.

List Making

Keep lists in handy places
for the adults and children in your family.

- ♥ grocery lists
- ♥ shopping lists
- ♥ holiday and birthday lists

Encourage all family members to add to the lists.

For the grocery store list, divide paper into sections. Label each section with a food category (vegetables, fruits, dairy products, meats, canned foods, frozen foods, etc.). To make shopping easier, family members can add foods to the list in the correct category.

Creative Recipes

Make a record of your family's favorite foods.

_____   _____

_____   _____

_____   _____

Write a favorite recipe below.

_____

_____

_____

_____

_____

To whom will you send recipes?

_____   _____

_____   _____

_____   _____

Creative Recipes

Encourage your children
to write recipes
for their favorite foods.

♥ Put recipe cards (or index cards), pencils, pens and markers in a handy location.

♥ Encourage your children to write recipes while you are in the kitchen together.

♥ Allow them to create their own recipes, writing how they think food dishes would be made.

♥ Save these creative recipe cards. Have fun rereading them occasionally.

♥ Use these recipe cards as gifts. Choose several of them, bundle them together with yarn, and give them to family members and friends as birthday and holiday gifts.

Sidewalk Stories

Write about your favorite sidewalk stories.
You won't forget them when the rain washes
them away!

_____

_____

_____

_____

_____

_____

_____

_____

_____

_____

Sidewalk Stories

Provide chalk for your children to use outdoors on the sidewalk and driveway.

Encourage your children to:

♥ Draw pictures

♥ Write messages

♥ Write stories

♥ Make maps

Leave messages for your children
on the sidewalk or driveway.

Song Rhymes

Write a family "Song Rhyme."
Sing it again and again.
Copy it and send it to family members and friends.

_____
(Choose a Tune)

_____
(Title of Your Family's Song Rhyme)

_____

_____

_____

_____

_____

_____

_____

For books containing song rhymes, see <u>SING ALONGS</u> and <u>SONG RHYMES</u> described in the back of this book.

Song Rhymes

Sing familiar tunes.

Add your own verses.

♥ Sing a familiar children's song.
  For example, sing "The Farmer in the Dell."

♥ Make up your own verses to the tune of "The Farmer in the Dell." For example, sing:
  We're going to visit the zoo.
  We're going to visit the zoo.
  We'll see the _____ and have some fun.
  We're going to visit the zoo.

♥ Have your children make a book, writing and illustrating your newly created song.

Other fun tunes:
Row, Row, Row Your Boat
Did You Ever See a Lassie?
Ten Little Indians
Twinkle, Twinkle, Little Star
Frere Jacques (Are You Sleeping?)
Do You Know the Muffin Man?
The Bear Went Over the Mountain
I'm a Little Teapot
The Wheels on the Bus
Old MacDonald Had a Farm
If You're Happy and You Know It, Clap Your Hands

K - W - L

Choose a topic that you want to study.
Complete the chart below.

What do we know about _____?

_____
_____
_____
_____
_____

What do we want to learn?

_____
_____
_____
_____
_____

What have we learned?

_____
_____
_____
_____
_____

K - W - L

What Do You <u>KNOW</u>?
What Do You <u>WANT</u> To Learn?
What Have You <u>LEARNED</u>?

Build background knowledge on topics that your children are interested in and topics being studied in school.

For example, if your children are interested in insects or are beginning to study insects in school, ask and discuss:

- ♥ What do you KNOW about insects?
- ♥ What do you WANT to learn about insects?
- ♥ What did you LEARN about insects?

ALPHABET ACTIVITIES

Young children make connections between letters, sounds and the meaning of print through exposure to print. Bring to life the print that surrounds your children. Read, write and talk about print. Notice what your children know about letters and sounds. Build on that knowledge.

Children's knowledge of letters and sounds is one of the best predictors of eventual success in reading. This knowledge does not come through drill and practice. It comes through continual exposure to meaningful print. Start early ... Notice the print that surrounds you every day.

Labels, Labels Everywhere

Search your home for labels
that begin with these letters.

a _____   n _____

b _____   o _____

c _____   p _____

d _____   q _____

e _____   r _____

f _____   s _____

g _____   t _____

h _____   u _____

i _____   v _____

j _____   w _____

k _____   x _____

l _____   y _____

m _____   z _____

Labels, Labels Everywhere

Help your children place labels on objects in your home.

door	kitchen	in -- out
chair	bedroom	up -- down
bookshelf	bathroom	floor -- ceiling
books	cereal	
table	bread	

♥ Read the labels every day.

♥ Play a guessing game, finding words that begin with certain letters and sounds. (Find all of the "s" words.)

♥ Find words that begin with the same letter or sound (bread and book)

♥ Add more labels every day.

Grocery Store Language

Complete the Grocery Store ABC's.
Each time you visit the grocery store,
look for new food names to add to the ABC's.

a _____   n _____

b _____   o _____

c _____   p _____

d _____   q _____

e _____   r _____

f _____   s _____

g _____   t _____

h _____   u _____

i _____   v _____

j _____   w _____

k _____   x _____

l _____   y _____

m _____   z _____

Grocery Store Language

The grocery store is full of words and language. Try some of these ideas when you visit the grocery store.

♥ Talk about the kinds of foods. For example, name fruits, vegetables, meats and dairy products. Name foods that come in cans, foods that need to be weighed, foods that are sweet and foods that are sour, foods that are hot and foods that are cold.

♥ Talk about the food labels. Notice the food labels that begin with different letters – "Banana" begins with b; "Carrot" begins with c; "Broccoli, banana and beans" begin the same.

♥ Think of words that rhyme with foods. For example, soup-coop, milk-silk, cheese-please, meat-heat.

♥ Sing or chant:
We're going shopping and what will we see?
We'll see lots of _____. That's what we'll see!

♥ Make a "Grocery Store Alphabet Book." Make one page for each letter of the alphabet. On each page, draw and label foods that begin with that letter. Take the book to the grocery store for your children to enjoy while shopping with you. (As they shop with their books, they will find more foods to add to their books!)

♥ Allow your children to take calculators to the grocery store. They can figure out the cost of your groceries before you get to the check-out.

Letters, Letters, Everywhere

Notice words that your children know. Write those words below. Family names and environmental print (mom, dad, Leslie, stop, Wal-Mart) help children learn letters and sounds.

a _____   n _____

b _____   o _____

c _____   p _____

d _____   q _____

e _____   r _____

f _____   s _____

g _____   t _____

h _____   u _____

i _____   v _____

j _____   w _____

k _____   x _____

l _____   y _____

m _____   z _____

Letters, Letters, Everywhere

Help your young children learn the names, shapes and sounds of the letters of the alphabet in these creative ways.

♥ Print large alphabet letters on separate pieces of paper. Allow your children to trace over the letters with their thumbprints. (Use a washable ink pad.)

♥ Print letters on large pieces of butcher paper. Turn on a flashlight and turn off the room lights. Have your children trace the letters using the flashlight. Put these letter posters on the walls in your children's bedrooms. They can use their flashlights every night.

♥ Give your children a box of toothpicks to form letters.

♥ Put shaving cream or whipped cream on a cookie sheet so that your children can make the letters and write some words. Also, this can be done with instant pudding or finger paints.

♥ Look for letters on cereal boxes and cans of food. Cut out these labels and have your children make an ABC book.

♥ Put magnetic letters on the refrigerator.

I Spy A-B-C's

List words and objects that begin
with each letter of the alphabet.

a _____   n _____

b _____   o _____

c _____   p _____

d _____   q _____

e _____   r _____

f _____   s _____

g _____   t _____

h _____   u _____

i _____   v _____

j _____   w _____

k _____   x _____

l _____   y _____

m _____   z _____

I Spy A-B-C's

When traveling in a car, watch for words and objects that begin with each letter of the alphabet.

Begin by writing the letters of the alphabet (A to Z) vertically on a piece of paper:

A ...
B ...
C ...
D ...
E ...

Then, fill in the blanks, naming words and objects that you see.

A ...
B ... bus (something you saw)
C ... cow (something you saw)
D ...
E ... Exit 135 (a road sign)
F ... Florida (license plate)

To add competition, keep score.
Put the person's name next to the word that he/she supplied.
Most important, have FUN!

I Spy License Plates

List license plate states
that begin with these letters.
(Make up names of states for
the letters that are not used.)

A _____   N _____

B _____   O _____

C _____   P _____

D _____   Q _____

E _____   R _____

F _____   S _____

G _____   T _____

H _____   U _____

I _____   V _____

J _____   W _____

K _____   X _____

L _____   Y _____

M _____   Z _____

I Spy License Plates

When traveling in a car, watch for
LICENSE PLATE STATES
that begin with each letter of the alphabet.

Begin by writing the letters of the alphabet (A to Z)
vertically on a piece of paper:

A ...
B ...
C ...
D ...
E ...
F ...
G ...

Then, fill in the blanks naming LICENSE PLATE STATES that
you see.

A ... Arizona
B ...
C ... California
D ...
E ...
F ... Florida
G ... Georgia

Categories

Name <u>FOODS</u> that begin with these letters.

s _____

t _____

m _____

b _____

a _____

j _____

Name <u>ANIMALS</u> that begin with these letters.

d _____

l _____

c _____

z _____

p _____

r _____

Categories

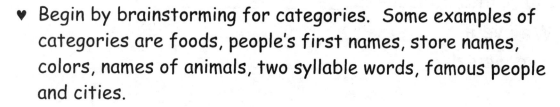

Brainstorm for words
that fit the category selected.

- ♥ Begin by brainstorming for categories. Some examples of categories are foods, people's first names, store names, colors, names of animals, two syllable words, famous people and cities.

- ♥ Write these on scraps of paper or just make a list of them.

- ♥ Next, choose 6 letters of the alphabet. Write these vertically on a piece of paper:

s _____

t _____

m _____

b _____

j _____

z _____

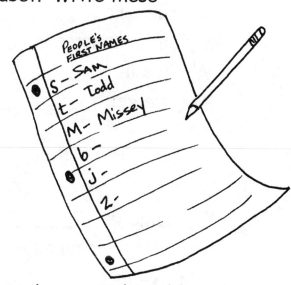

- ♥ Next, choose one category. For example, you might select "people's first names."

- ♥ Finally, fill in the above letters with "people's first names."

- ♥ Have fun selecting new categories and new letters to continue playing this game.

My Name is Annie

Play this word game.
Record your ideas below.

My name is _____.
My brother's name is _____.
We live in _____.
And we sell _____.

My name is _____.
My sister's name is _____.
We live in _____.
And we sell _____.

My name is _____.
My brother's name is _____.
We live in _____.
And we sell _____.

My Name is Annie

Use words that begin with the same letter of the alphabet to complete the following story:

My name is _____.
My brother's (or sister's) name is _____.
We live in _____.
And we sell _____.

Here's an example:

My name is <u>Mark</u>.
My sister's name is <u>Marcia</u>.
We live in <u>Minnesota</u>.
And we sell <u>marshmallows</u>.

To play as a group game:

Write the letters of the alphabet on small scraps of paper. Have each person draw a letter. That would be the letter that they would need to use for their story.

READING AND WRITING ...

BEYOND BOOKS AND STORIES

Expose your children to other forms of print.
Create in them an interest and curiosity that drives
them to make reading and writing natural
experiences in their everyday lives.

Map Reading

Plan trips and vacations or just pretend. Provide your children with maps and travel brochures for their leisure reading and planning.

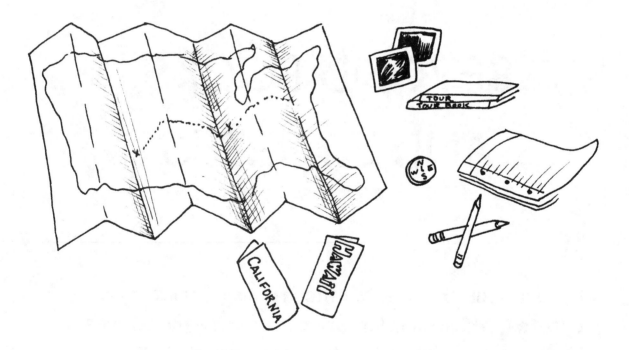

Maps and travel brochures are available through:

♥ Travel agencies

♥ Libraries

♥ Your city's Chamber of Commerce

Coupon Collections

Save money and encourage reading
at the same time!

♥ Design a special box for your coupon collection.

♥ Encourage all family members to add coupons
to the box.

♥ Once a week, encourage children to sort coupons.

When you are ready to go shopping:

♥ Select the coupons that you want to use.
♥ Ask your children to estimate how much you will save by using
the selected coupons.
♥ Have them add up the exact amount. (Using a small calculator
makes this a fun task.)

Restaurant Reading

Check out the menu ...

♥ Read the menu to your children.

♥ Have them read parts of the menu to you.

♥ Find words that are repeated ... How many times can you find the words "hamburger, dessert, french fries?"

♥ How many words can you find that begin with the same letter ... How many T words? M words? Words that begin like your first name?

♥ What is the longest word on the menu?

♥ What is the shortest word?

♥ What is your favorite word on the menu?

♥ What foods do you like? What foods do you NOT like?

Cereal Box Reading

Cereal boxes provide
lots of reading and
entertainment for children
(and adults, too).

♥ Place several cereal boxes on the table at
breakfast time. Children will enjoy the stories,
cartoons, puzzles and messages.

♥ When cereal boxes are empty, save them. They
can be placed on a bookshelf or toy shelf.
Children can continue to read them and items
can be stored inside the empty cereal boxes.

♥ Cover a cereal box with white paper. (Ask the
grocer for some white butcher paper.)
Encourage your children to design their own
cereal box. They can create their own name for
their cereal, describe it and illustrate it. They
can add other creative information to their
cereal box.

Comics to Clip

Encourage each person in the family to save their favorite comics and cartoons.

♥ Read the comics and cartoons.

♥ Write new captions for them.

♥ Sort them into categories (animal cartoons, school cartoons, family cartoons, etc.).

♥ Hang them up around the house.

♥ Send a comic or cartoon to others when you send cards and presents.

Jokes and Riddles

Jokes and riddles can provide entertainment, conversation and reading practice.

♥ Tear apart (or photocopy) your favorite joke and riddle books so that each joke/riddle is on a separate piece of paper.

♥ Put them in a box labeled "Jokes and Riddles."

Have fun reading and rereading jokes and riddles. This can be done in the car, while you are preparing a meal, on the telephone and whenever you have a few spare minutes.

Writing Toolbox

Create a writing toolbox that holds the supplies that your children will want to use when writing letters, stories, or making books.

You might want to include some of the following items:

- ♥ paper (blank and lined)
- ♥ envelopes
- ♥ post cards
- ♥ postage stamps
- ♥ pencils, pens, erasers
- ♥ markers, crayons
- ♥ decorative stamps and stamp pad
- ♥ stapler
- ♥ yarn
- ♥ ruler
- ♥ hole punch
- ♥ pencil sharpener
- ♥ tape and glue

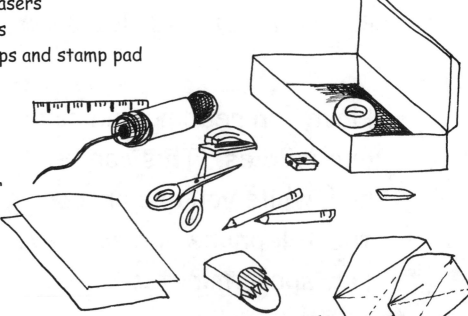

Pen Pals ...
Writing Buddies

Find a pen pal for each of your children. The pen pal might be a grandma, grandpa, aunt, uncle, friend or neighbor.

Write letters to each other regularly.

In your letters, ask a few questions.

Share photos.

♥ Younger children (pre-writers) can draw a picture and tell you what to write.

Photo Albums

Have your children design a family memory book.

♥ Give your children an empty photo album, some family photos and some color markers. Encourage your children to put photos in the album and add captions.

♥ Just a sentence or two about each photo will bring back special memories for years to come.

♥ When photos are not available, children can draw pictures of special people and special events.

Magazine Writing

- ♥ Collect a variety of interesting pictures from magazines. Place the pictures in a flat box.

- ♥ Encourage your children to select a picture and write about it. The picture may remind them of something they have done or somewhere they have gone. Or they might want to create a story about the picture.

- ♥ Set aside time for family story writing. Have each family member select a picture from the box and write about it.

- ♥ After writing, trade pictures. Write about someone else's picture. Then compare stories.

- ♥ To add some fun, have one person read each story. Others can guess who wrote each story.

Magnet Fun

Place magnetic letters on the refrigerator.

Magnetic letters can be purchased at toy stores and discount stores. With very young children, place them up high on the refrigerator or put them on the refrigerator only when the older children are using them.

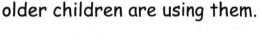

Use magnetic letters:

♥ Write messages to your children.

♥ Spell out special words and names.

♥ Practice spelling words.

♥ Make word families (bat, cat, fat, rat, that).

♥ Make crossword puzzle word designs.

Have fun with the magnetic letters.
Just having them there will encourage your children
to play with words and messages.

Notes ...Anytime and Anywhere

Write short notes to your children.
Place them in "surprise" places.

Place notes in:

- ♥ lunch boxes
- ♥ book bags
- ♥ under pillows
- ♥ on the bathroom mirror
- ♥ on the bedroom door
- ♥ on and in the refrigerator
- ♥ under dinner plates
- ♥ in the cookie jar
- ♥ in the car
- ♥ in shirt and pant pockets

Keep note paper and scotch tape handy.
Your children will want to write back
to you!

Telephone Messages

Put a message pad and pencil next to each telephone.

Have your children follow a regular procedure when they answer the telephone and take messages. (At first, you might need to write the procedure on a piece of paper for them to follow.)

♥ Answer the telephone with a greeting.

♥ If the person is not home, find out --

> WHO called
>
> WHAT they need
>
> WHAT their phone number is
>
> WHEN the person can call back

♥ Finish the telephone call in a polite way (Thank you for calling; Have a good day; Good bye).

MORE LITERACY ACTIVITIES

Immerse your children in literacy experiences. Notice what you do with reading and writing. Expose your children to those same activities. Explain to them what you are doing and why you are engaged in that literacy experience.

Children learn best through their role models -- you and significant others. Also, they learn best by being actively engaged in learning experiences.

Conversation, Singing and Rhyming

When did you first begin to speak to your children?

From the moment your children are born, surround them with language.

Talk, sing, rhyme and listen --

- ♥ as you dress your children
- ♥ as you prepare meals
- ♥ when you are traveling in the car
- ♥ when you are in a store
- ♥ when you are walking
- ♥ when you are at the playground
- ♥ when you are waiting for an appointment

Children begin to learn language by listening. Then they speak. The language that they hear and speak becomes the foundation for reading and writing. So surround them with language.

Sing, Rhyme and Rap

Children benefit from hearing songs, rhymes and rhythmic language.

♥ Help your young children learn nursery rhymes. Say them, chant them, rap them and sing them.

♥ Teach your children familiar children's songs.

♥ A book from your school or public library will have many popular songs and rhymes that children enjoy.

♥ Repeating and memorizing songs and rhymes help children become comfortable and creative with language.

Give a Gift of a Book

A book may be the BEST PRESENT that you can give because ...

- ♥ When you give a book as a gift, you are saying that you value reading.
- ♥ You serve as a positive role model, showing your children that you appreciate books.
- ♥ Your children will read the book again and again.
- ♥ Children love books.

Instead of buying greeting cards for your children's birthdays,
BUY A BOOK!
Write a message and sign your name on the inside cover.
It is guaranteed to be a "card" that lasts a long, long time!

Bible Stories

Bible stories help families
to develop values and virtues.

As families read about God and
about Bible characters,
they understand:

- ♥ the unconditional love that God has for us.
- ♥ how God has a perfect plan for each person's life.
- ♥ how we are secure in His love.
- ♥ the virtues of faithfulness, compassion, truthfulness,
  honesty, trust, etc. that are displayed through the
  characters in the Bible.

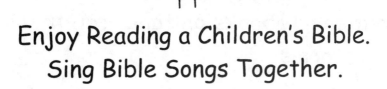

Enjoy Reading a Children's Bible.
Sing Bible Songs Together.

Books on Tape

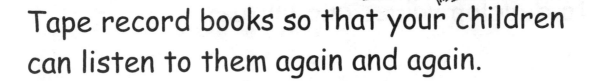

Tape record books so that your children can listen to them again and again.

- ♥ When you are reading to your children, turn on the tape recorder. Tape record the story. Put the book and the cassette tape in a plastic baggie for future listening and reading.

- ♥ When you tape record a book, have your children make an audible sound when it is time to turn the page (clap hands, tap table, ring a bell). When they listen to the tape, the sound will clue them to turn the page.

- ♥ Have relatives and friends tape record books for your children. This is especially meaningful when the tape recording comes through the mail from "someone special."

- ♥ If you are away from your children at bedtime, leave out some "books on tape" for their bedtime stories.

Books and Tapes in the Car

Tape record books while you are reading to your children. Tape record songs while you are singing together.

Take the tapes and books with you when you are in the car. Have fun listening, reading and singing together.

Playing School

Most children learn
to "play school" naturally.
They have the "tools" around them
so they begin to play.

Provide your children with:

♥ books

♥ writing tools (paper, pencils, markers, stapler)

♥ chalkboard and chalk

♥ marker board and markers

♥ flash cards, for math and reading

♥ a table or desk

♥ a pointer for the "teacher"

♥ a clock and a calendar

Spell As You Go

Practice your children's spelling
words while driving in the car.

♥ Take your children's spelling words with you in the car.
Have them copy the list and keep this extra copy in the car.

♥ Take turns spelling words as you run daily errands in the car.

♥ Add to the words by rhyming them and spelling the rhyming
words.

♥ If the word has more than one part (syllable), have your
children spell one part at a time.

♥ Talk about what each word means. Use the words in
sentences.

Television

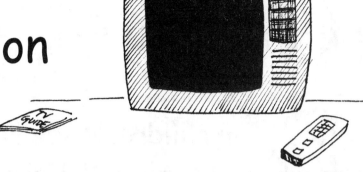

♥ Limit your children's television viewing.
♥ Be selective about what they watch.
♥ Set aside more time for reading and writing than you set aside for television, videos and video games.

Suggestions for limiting and selecting television shows:

♥ Allow your children a certain number of minutes of TV each day (or each week). Expect them to select the shows and list them, along with the number of minutes for each show.
♥ Encourage your children to use the television guide to select what they want to watch.
♥ Encourage your children to choose some educational television shows. Enjoy watching these shows together.

Take the plunge:
Turn off the television for two weeks.
Provide books, writing materials, board games, outdoor activities and conversation.
Notice what happens.

AVAILABLE MATERIALS FROM LITERACY LINKS

NOW IN PAPERBACK

SING ALONGS:
HELPING CHILDREN LEARN TO READ

**FULL-COLOR COVER
8 x 11 BOOK
96 PAGES**

SING ALONGS: HELPING CHILDREN LEARN TO READ is perfect for emergent and beginning readers, for use in school and at home. This paperback book combines song and rhyme to reinforce pre-reading and beginning reading strategies and vocabulary.

INCLUDES:
- ♥ 23 song rhymes, illustrated and in primary print
- ♥ Tips for parents and educators on how to use each song rhyme to encourage good beginning reading habits (one page of tips for each song rhyme)
- ♥ One page of word cards for each song rhyme
- ♥ Easy-to-understand explanation of how children learn to read and what can be done at home to help children become good readers

Use SING ALONGS: HELPING CHILDREN LEARN TO READ to allow literacy experiences to flow from school to home.

TO ORDER, CONTACT
LITERACY LINKS ♦ 8 Larkmoor Drive ♦ Glen Carbon, IL 62034
(618) 288-4999 ♦ http://www.literacylinks.com

Blackline Masters
Available through Literacy Links

Unlike the paperback books, these blackline masters can be reproduced.

♥ However, one set of blackline masters PER SCHOOL needs to be purchased. (Copyright permission allows purchasing school to reproduce blackline masters for use in their school.)

POEMS AND NURSERY RHYMES

A COLLECTION OF 60 ILLUSTRATED POEMS AND NURSERY PHYMES in primary print can be used in the classroom and at home. The poems are ideal for pre-school through grade 2 children. Choral read, reread, and partner read the "poem of the week." Then send the illustrated copy of the poem home for children "to perform" in front of their parents. This is a no-cost way to provide a literacy link between school and home. Included are suggestions for using poetry to reinforce language development, phonemic awareness, sight vocabulary, and to boost self confidence and self esteem. Also included are letters to parents explaining how to use poetry at home.

SONG RHYMES

COMBINE SONG AND RHYME to reinforce pre-reading and beginning reading strategies and vocabulary. Simple poems, in primary print, are set to the tunes of familiar songs. They are attractively illustrated and reproducible for use in the classroom and at home. A page of word bank cards accompanies each of the 45 song rhymes. Enjoy using these Song Rhymes to encourage literacy experiences at home.

PARENT HANDBOOKS AND STRATEGY SHEETS

REPRODUCIBLE PARENT HANDBOOKS can be assembled to use with parents of pre-school through grade 3 children. These handbooks provide excellent direction on topics to discuss and demonstrate during parent gatherings. Each handbook contains information and strategies about reading aloud to children, reading together, rereading books and finding time for reading. Echo Reading, Fill in the Gap, and Clues for Decoding Unknown Words are among the popular strategies that are explained in the handbooks. Specific ideas for encouraging reading, writing and spelling at home are included. Preschool and Kindergarten Parent Handbooks include sections entitled Letter and Sound Recognition Through the Magic of Books, Magnetboard Fun, Writing Opportunities and Alphabet Fun. **STRATEGY SHEETS** list simplified suggestions that encourage family literacy experiences. They are printed "bookmark style" with 2-3 strategies per page. Copy them, cut them apart and send them home.

SPONTANEOUS LITERACY EXPERIENCES

SIMPLE SUGGESTIONS OF READING, WRITING, SPEAKING AND LISTENING EXPERIENCES that families can engage in spontaneously. Reproducible pages can be sent home on a weekly basis to remind parents of practical ways to "smuggle" literacy experiences into their everyday lives. Each page is attractively illustrated. Use throughout the school – in the classroom, library, and in school newsletters.

READING, WRITING, RHYMES AND WORDS

A collection of **SPIN-OFF ACTIVITIES FOR 20 POPULAR CHILDREN'S BOOKS**. Books selected have repetitious phrases and/or cumulative story lines. Reproducible pages allow children to reread key parts of the book (repetitious phrases), to write their own books following the author's pattern, and to study key words using the word bank cards included. Excellent for use at school AND home. Titles include I Went Walking, Draw Me a Star, It Looked Like Spilt Milk, If the Dinosaurs Came Back, Quick as a Cricket, Wheels on the Bus, Eency Weency Spider, Who Stole the Cookies, Lions and Gorillas, When This Box is Full. Books are NOT included but can be ordered in paperback from publishers listed on enclosed book list.

HIGH FREQUENCY WORD CARDS AND CONSONANT CARDS

HIGH FREQUENCY SIGHT VOCABULARY WORDS (220 Dolch words) are arranged with 10 word and sentence cards per page (22 pages totally). Words are in large, bold type followed by a sentence in primary print. Copy and send home for parents and children to practice. Use at parent conferences and meetings to demonstrate reading, spelling and writing high frequency words and to demonstrate use of context clues. Also included are letters to parents. **CONSONANT CARDS** are picture and word cards that can be reproduced for use at school and home. Set includes one page per consonant letter. Each page contains four words (and pictures) in large primary print. When cut apart, these cards allow children the opportunity to practice letter/sound recognition, beginning sounds, ending sounds, and other aspects of phonemic awareness. Letter to parents is included.